THE Change Your Life BOOK

Bill O'Hanlon

Health Communications, Inc.
Deerfield Beach, Florida

www.hcibooks.com

Library of Congress Cataloging-in-Publication Data

O'Hanlon, William Hudson.
   The change your life book / Bill O'Hanlon.
      p. cm.
   ISBN 978-0-7573-1631-9 (pbk.)
   ISBN 0-7573-1631-X (pbk.)
   ISBN 978-0-7573-1632-6 (ebook)
   ISBN 0-7573-1632-8 (ebook)
     1. Change (Psychology)   2. Habit.   3. Conduct of life—Psychological
aspects.   I. Title.
   BF637.C4O434 2012
   158—dc23

                                         2011053059

Publisher: Health Communications, Inc.
          3201 S.W. 15th Street
          Deerfield Beach, FL 33442–8190

Cover design by Larissa Hise Henoch
Interior design and formatting by Lawna Patterson Oldfield

To **Helen**, whose one **change** in **my life** made **all** the **difference**.

Contents

Part 2: Change the Viewing Tips

Part 3: Change the Setting Tips

Introduction

In 1999, I had a book published that was featured on *Oprah* called *Do One Thing Different*. The book was well received and the biggest seller of any of my previous books, in large part due to the exposure from being on Oprah. The publishers were happily surprised and promptly arranged for me to do forty radio interviews. Most of these interviews were less than ten minutes long, and I had to work hard to distill the book's message in the brief time allotted.

After doing those interviews, I wished I could write the book over again. I had focused my thinking and the message so well by then that I knew I could write a different and better book. In a lighthearted moment, I thought of the book featured in the 1991 comedy movie *What About Bob?* The book in that movie was called *Baby Steps*. This book embodies the idea of taking small steps to make bigger, more significant changes. My goal as I wrote *The Change Your Life Book* was to quickly communicate the lighthearted and fun flavor these small change tips have.

The message of this book is simple: It is difficult to make big or dramatic changes. It is much easier to make small or simple ones. But even those small, simple changes can sometimes result in big shifts. You never know which small change will have a big effect, so as you read through this book, try a number of the suggestions to find the ones that work for you.

There are generally three ways you can make changes in your life:

1. **Change the Doing:** Change your actions, interactions, and how you speak about situations or experiences.

2. **Change the Viewing:** Change the focus of your attention and the meanings or interpretations you bring to situations or experiences.

3. **Change the Setting:** Change locations or other contexts and discover something new.

Of course, if you change one of these areas, it often shifts the other areas. For example, if you experiment with staying silent when you would usually say something (Change the Doing Tip #9), you might observe something you had never noticed before (which changes the Viewing) and others might respond differently to you with your untypical behavior (which changes the Context).

This book provides fifty-two small shifts you can make to change your life. If you experiment with one a week for the next year, and you are sincere in your efforts to change, it's highly likely you will have a better life with better relationships. No guarantees, of course; life doesn't come with guarantees. But people who tried these tips when they were only available as weekly e-mails found that at least a few of them made a positive impact on their lives, so I am confident they will have a positive impact on yours as well.

I have arranged these tips into the categories listed above, but feel free to skip around and try any that appeal to you. Keep an open mind and have fun. Hopefully they won't turn into obligations or burdens but will be interesting learning experiences. Remember that these tips may not necessarily be the right suggestions for you, so treat them as possibilities rather than commands. If they fit (and work), use them, but if something I suggest doesn't fit or work for you, trust yourself and ignore what I suggest.

Bill O'Hanlon
Santa Fe, New Mexico
May 2011

PART 1:

Change
the Doing
Tips

Change the Mode of Expression

Everything that is done in the
world is done by hope.

—Martin Luther

Sometimes changing how you express something can change the situation or the experience of it. For example, a couple could stop their oral argument and write down everything they want to say during the argument, or they could record their responses on a tape recorder in a different room for their partner to play back in private and then record a response to what their partner has recorded. Or instead of writing an e-mail to someone you are upset with, pick up the phone and call them.

Instead of writing an e-mail to someone you are upset with, pick up the phone and call them.

That leads to this suggestion: Change the mode of expression used in some problem situation. Determine your usual mode of expression and switch to any other mode as an experiment.

Externalize Problems or Haunting Memories

The future is an infinite succession of presents, and to live now as we think human beings should live, in defiance of all that is bad around us, is itself a marvelous victory.

—Howard Zinn

I once had a client who was anorexic. When we discussed it, she revealed that while she was eating, these critical voices in her head were saying terrible things about her, such as "You are ugly. You are fat. You have no self-control," and so on. I discovered that she basically had the critical litany memorized. I suggested she record the litany and play it back as she sat down to eat. She found that putting it on tape essentially nullified the effect of the critical voice.

In a similar vein, I once heard Bob Simon, a television correspondent who had been captured and ill-treated by the Iraqis during the first Gulf War, tell an interviewer that he suffered post-traumatic nightmares and flashbacks until he wrote a book about his experience. After that, he said, "The experience was in the book, so it no longer haunted me."

That leads to this suggestion: Externalize any recurring, critical, or torturous thoughts, memories, or voices by writing them out, recording them onto an audiotape or videotape, or putting them into some other external form (such as an artwork).

Baby Steps, Bob, Baby Steps

Habit is habit and not to be
flung out of the window by any man,
but coaxed downstairs
a step at a time.

—Mark Twain

I used to procrastinate doing my taxes. Every year I would file for extension after extension and still not get them done. Finally, over time, I came up with a strategy that worked. I would spend five minutes each week at a designated time (Monday morning first thing) going through my stacks of disorganized papers and sorting them into more organized smaller stacks. First, I just put all the tax-related papers into one stack. Then, in subsequent sessions, I would sort this stack into smaller stacks of categories within my tax preparation work. A few years ago, my accountant almost fell over when I gave her all my records in January.

Finally, over time, I came up with a strategy that worked.

This suggestion is simple then: Identify something you have been procrastinating about or that you are having trouble with. Break whatever you need to do into smaller pieces or chunks of time, and make progress on it every day this week.

The **Expiration-Dated** Box

Look, walking on water
wasn't built in a day.

—Jack Kerouac

This tip is for those who keep lots of stuff and won't organize it or get rid of it. I read about this idea years ago, so it's not original, but I don't remember where I got it. It has worked for me, since I'm a bit of a pack rat. I tend to hold on to articles and other papers that pile up in my office, the living room, the kitchen—any flat surface. (Someone once joked that all flat surfaces should be removed from my surroundings, and only A-frame tables should be allowed.)

> It has worked for me, since I'm a bit of a pack rat.

Get a friend or family member to take stacks of paper and put them into a box. Label the box (with big markers) for a date one year from the time that the paper goes into the box. If the box hasn't been sorted, emptied, filed, and organized by the date on the box, the friend or family member is to throw the box in the trash.

Stop Doing **Something**

Drawing on my fine command
of language, I said nothing.

—Robert Benchley

Sometimes, instead of doing something in a new way or doing a new thing, we need to stop doing something to make a change. When writing my first books, I found I procrastinated and avoided writing. The main time waster I had was reading several news magazines each week. Of course, most of the information was redundant. I decided to let all my magazine subscriptions lapse, and when the books were completed, I would never again resubscribe to those news weeklies (I still got news from the daily paper, the radio, and the television).

- What do you need to stop doing to find more time or change the quality of your life?

- What habit or action could you stop to improve your relationships?

- What habit or action could you stop to improve your health?

Stretch
Your Brain

It takes courage to push yourself to places
that you have never been before . . .
to test your limits . . . to break through
barriers. And the day came when the risk
[it took] to remain tight in the bud was more
painful than the risk it took to bloom.

—Anaïs Nin

Recent research has reported that learning new things as you age can help prevent mental deterioration and perhaps even stave off Alzheimer's and senility. Over the past year, I have been deliberately getting myself to learn all about the Internet, something that is a real stretch for me because I am not very technical and have been a bit intimidated by this resource. I was determined to find ways to get my message and ideas out to a wider audience and also to create content that wouldn't require me to put in more time to do so. You are reading one of the fruits of this new learning. Before these tips were gathered into a book, they were e-mail tips that were delivered via e-mail by autoresponder, a technology I didn't know about or how to use before this past year.

So this tip involves deliberately seeking out new learning experiences. Find something that you want to know more about or learn how to do that seems like a stretch to you, and spend time regularly (every day, every week, every month) pushing yourself to engage in the learning process. Find teachers or mentors in your area of interest. Get audios, videos, or books on the subject. Or just plunge in and get started, being willing not to know and to make mistakes.

Enjoy Your **Food**

Every action taken, from the moment
we switch off the alarm clock in the morning
to the way we write a line of poetry or
design a product, has the potential to
change the world, leave it cold with indifference,
or perhaps more commonly, nudge it
infinitesimally in the direction of good and evil.

—David Whyte

I came across a study in Barry Glassner's book, *The Gospel of Food: Everything You Think You Know About Food Is Wrong,* (HarperCollins, 2007), that seems to show that when we eat with pleasure (rather than with guilt or fear, as many of us do), we get more out of the food nutritionally. Using groups of Swedish women and Thai women, researchers had the women eat a spicy Thai meal (rice and vegetables spiced with hot chilies, fish sauce, and coconut milk) that most of the Swedish women found overly spicy. It was discovered that the Thai women absorbed more iron from the meal than the Swedish women did—in some women, up to 50 percent more.

When we eat for pleasure, we get more out of the food nutritionally.

Then the researchers had the same groups of women eat food that appealed more to the Swedish palate (hamburgers, potatoes, and beans), and they found that the Swedish women absorbed more iron from the food than the Thai women. Then they blended all of the ingredients of the original Thai meal, which was packed with nutrients, into a liquid and fed it to the same Thai women. Not only did the Thai women complain about having to drink the nasty liquid, but tests showed that they did not absorb as much iron as they had with the original meal. The researchers proved that people absorb more nutrients from food that they enjoy eating.

What might this mean for you and some small change you can make? Instead of eating on the basis of some food rules or the fear of getting fat, try eating something you really like for one meal a day without guilt and with pleasure and enjoyment.

Your "**Not-to-Do**" List

The one thing you need to know about sustained individual success: Discover what you don't like doing and stop doing it.

—Marcus Buckingham, *The One Thing You Need to Know*

One of the keys to success is to have a good "not-to-do" list. Make a list of things you would like to stop doing or do less of, then take steps to do less of that stuff.

Perhaps you can change your circumstances so you can stop doing certain things. Or perhaps you could hire someone else (with money or by barter) to take over things you dislike doing. For example, I left my job at a community mental health center to start a private practice because I disliked the number of (to my mind) useless meetings and all the paperwork. I liked the therapy part of my work the best.

> Make a list of things you would like to stop doing or do less of, then take steps to do less of that stuff.

Silence Can Be **Golden**

Speech is conveniently located
midway between thought and action,
where it often substitutes for both.

—John Andrew Holmes

I admire the late philosopher, poet, geometer, and designer R. Buckminster (Bucky) Fuller. He contemplated committing suicide but decided not to, because he believed the universe doesn't make anything without a purpose. But he didn't yet know what his purpose was. So he decided to be silent and think about it. He told his (long-suffering and always supportive) wife of his plan. She agreed, but neither of them knew at the time that he would remain silent for years. When he finally spoke, he had lots to say and found his purpose for living in those silent years.

> When he finally spoke, he had lots to say and found his purpose for living in those silent years.

How about trying an experiment? Be silent for a day—longer if you can swing it—and no distractions, if you can manage that as well. Just be with yourself in silence. I wonder what you'll discover, if anything? I wonder what will change as a result, if anything?

Don't
Be **Yourself**

When you're through changing, you're through.

—Bruce Barton

In any relationship, people seem to fall into patterns. One of the patterns is that we routinely do things that annoy those who are around us for any length of time. Some of our usual actions irritate them.

> If you never offer to pay for lunch, grab the check as soon as it arrives.

So your assignment, should you accept it, is to note anything that you do regularly that someone you are in a relationship with finds upsetting and do something that blows their minds because it is unlike how you usually behave in that area.

For example, if you never take out the garbage without being hounded, take it out before being reminded. Or, if you are routinely late, show up early or on time several times. If you never offer to pay for lunch, grab the check as soon as it arrives. You get the point. Your spouse/partner/friend/parent/child/coworker will think a clone has taken over your body. The person looks like you but doesn't act anything like you. Leave them scratching their heads and wondering who that clone is. And, if you can, leave them delighted.

The **Hard** Thing

Do the difficult things while they are
easy and do the great things while
they are small. A journey of a
thousand miles must begin with a single step.

—Lao-tzu

For the next week, first thing in the morning, do a little bit of the hardest task you have to do: something you've been avoiding, something that is a bit beyond you or is confusing, something you hate to do but know you need to get done, and so on.

You might choose some bottleneck task that could move you forward on some long-standing goal or dream. You might choose something that will begin to complete some unfinished business or let you move on from something or someone.

Think hard.
Make a list.
Get going.

Think hard. Make a list. Get going. You have nothing to lose but a little time and some psychic detritus.

One **Drawer** at a **Time**

Nature abhors a vacuum. And so do I.

—Anne Gibbons

This week, choose one drawer to go through and organize, throw away, or donate unneeded items. That's it. Short and sweet. (And if you are one of those people whose drawers are already totally organized and cleared out, good for you. But the rest of us find you obnoxious, so don't flaunt it.)

That's it.
Short and sweet.

Completion Brings **Energy**

I like work: it fascinates me.
I can sit and look at it for hours.

—Jerome K. Jerome

I attended a time management seminar some years ago and the instructor made a point that has stuck with me: Completion brings energy (and the correlate, incompletion, drains energy). Of course, being a possibility-oriented kind of guy, I would restate it: Completion can bring energy and incompletion can drain energy.

> Completion can bring energy and incompletion can drain energy.

But here's the idea, which I have noticed is true for me more often than not. Say you have an unpaid bill sitting on your kitchen table. Every time you glance at that bill, it takes just a little of your energy and attention. Once you pay it, no energy and time drain from you.

Or, you have something on your mind that you need to remember. It is draining just a little of the attention/energy that you have available in your day or in your life. Writing down the task or what you want to remember in a place where you know you will see it again when you need to be reminded of it decreases or stops that drain. These drains can come from things we need to communicate to other people, things we need to clean up, tasks we need to do, bills we need to pay, and so on.

So, this brings us to this change tip: Notice one incomplete item per day this next week and either complete it or create a system to remember it and retrieve it when needed. As video blogger, artist, and entrepreneur Bre Pettis has written, "Done is the engine of more." Getting things completed can bring energy to do whatever else you want to do.

The **Value** of **Doing Nothing**

Don't underestimate the value of
Doing Nothing, of just going along,
listening to all the things you can't hear,
and not bothering.

—Winnie the Pooh

Most people are so busy these days that this tip suggests that you simply schedule one day in the next few weeks in which you do nothing productive, but only fun or flaky things. One whole day. You may have to wrestle with guilt. You may have to deal with anxiety. You may have to stand up to pressure from others for you to be productive or to do something you "should" do.

It could be an interesting experiment, though. Or a preview of days to come.

> Schedule one day in the next few weeks in which you do nothing productive.

Going **Ape** in Your **Relationship**

It's weird . . . people say they're not like apes.
Now how do you explain football then?

—Mitch Hedberg

Some years ago, I saw a book in a bookstore called *Going Ape: How to Stop Talking About Your Relationship and Start Enjoying It* (Julius Rosen, Contemporary Books, 1990). It was a self-help book for relationships, and the basic idea was that we often get into trouble in relationships when we use words and misunderstand one another.

Since much of our emotional communication is nonverbal anyway, this author suggested that when there is trouble in a relationship or you want to communicate something emotional, restrict yourself to using only methods available to apes. I shared this with a romantic partner of mine once and we routinely started using it to good effect.

When I had messed up and done something she didn't like, I would make little whiny noises and grab her hand and rub it on top of my head (I borrowed this from a Tarzan movie I saw). She and I both found she softened with this approach, as opposed to arguing or talking about it. She used her own nonverbal ways of communicating when things got tough, and I responded well.

So, get creative. Go ape (in a good way). Go bananas. Test it out and find out what happens.

Getting **Up** on the **Right** **Side** of the Bed

Human salvation lies in the hands
of the creatively maladjusted.

—Martin Luther King Jr.

I have a friend named Chris who told me a charming story about when she first adopted kids. Chris had never been a morning person but now had to be, since her kids got up and needed to be attended to and cared for.

After some time, she found herself being cranky in the mornings. One day her husband remarked that she must have gotten up on the wrong side of the bed. Thinking about this principle of changing small things, it suddenly occurred to her, *Maybe I did get up on the wrong side of the bed!*

The next morning, she deliberately crawled out on her husband's side of the bed and found herself amused. It started her morning in a whole different mood. It worked for quite a while, then one morning she found herself getting cranky again. So the next morning, she crawled off the front of the bed instead. That worked!

Now, can you get creative and come up with some small change in habit or pattern to change something that is not working in your daily life? Write me at Bill@billohanlon. com and tell me if you come up with something that works. I love those stories!

READER/CUSTOMER CARE SURVEY

HEMG

We care about your opinions! Please take a moment to fill out our online Reader Survey at **http://survey.hcibooks.com**. As a **"THANK YOU"** you will receive a **VALUABLE INSTANT COUPON** towards future book purchases as well as a **SPECIAL GIFT** available only online! Or, you may mail this card back to us.

First Name		MI.		Last Name

Address				

State		Zip		Email		City

1. Gender
❑ Female   ❑ Male

2. Age
❑ 8 or younger
❑ 9-12   ❑ 13-16
❑ 17-20   ❑ 21-30
❑ 31+

3. Did you receive this book as a gift?
❑ Yes   ❑ No

4. Annual Household Income
❑ under $25,000
❑ $25,000 - $34,999
❑ $35,000 - $49,999
❑ $50,000 - $74,999
❑ over $75,000

5. What are the ages of the children living in your house?
❑ 0 - 14   ❑ 15+

6. Marital Status
❑ Single
❑ Married
❑ Divorced
❑ Widowed

Comments
_____
_____
_____
_____
_____
_____

BUSINESS REPLY MAIL

FIRST-CLASS MAIL   PERMIT NO 45   DEERFIELD BEACH, FL

POSTAGE WILL BE PAID BY ADDRESSEE

Health Communications, Inc.
3201 SW 15th Street
Deerfield Beach FL 33442-9875

Life Is Full of Letting Go (or Not)

All the art of living lies in a fine
mingling of letting go and holding on.

—Havelock Ellis

How about this as a small change plan? Let go of or get rid of one object per day for the next week. Or if you are already organized, let go of one resentment this week. Just decide/choose to forgo resentment, hatred, and wishing the person bad things in their life.

Let go of or get rid of one object per day for the next week.

The **Hard** Conversation

Most conversations are simply monologues delivered in the presence of a witness.

—Margaret Millar

Have one hard conversation per week.

Some of us avoid the hard conversations because they are (or could be) uncomfortable. The other person might be unpleasant, might lie, might get upset with us, might try to weasel out of something. We might have to say things that are hard for us to say or that might make us look or feel bad. We might have to do something we are very afraid of.

Still, not having those conversations often makes things worse: lost friendships, lost money, lost opportunities, even lawsuits or violence might result from avoided conversations. So consider what conversations you have been avoiding and, if there are any, seek out the person/people with whom you need to have them (in person and by phone/Skype are best, because nonverbal communication is important in difficult and challenging conversations).

Once you are having the conversation, be willing to openly listen and be surprised by what you hear. And as much as is possible, tell the truth from your side of things, but don't insist that your truth is *the way it is*. A true conversation, even when challenging, is always two-sided.

Chip Away at **Unhelpful** and **Limiting** Habits

It is better to take many small steps in
the right direction than to make a great leap
forward only to stumble backward.

—Chinese proverb

Identify the typical habits that limit you, hold you back, or cause trouble in your life. Mine include procrastination, avoidance, and messiness. Choose one of those habits and begin to chip away at it. How?

You might write down and commit to doing one thing every day or every week to challenge or chip away at that habit. For me, that would be to do one avoided/procrastinated thing per day, clean up one thing from a messy pile of stuff, or choose one drawer to clean out/ organize.

Tell others out loud or on your blog that you are committed to changing that habit.

Go public: Tell others out loud or on your blog that you are committed to changing that habit, and detail your plan. Tell them you will report back and give them permission to remind you or check with you about that commitment.

Use whatever clever ways you can think of to challenge or chip away at these limiting habits that have been holding you back from your dreams or a better, more satisfying life.

Doggedly Determined

I think dogs are the most amazing creatures;
they give unconditional love. For me
they are the role model for being alive.

—Gilda Radner

Continuing the animal theme from another change tip (Tip #15: Going Ape), I am reminded of a case we had at the therapy group practice in which I worked some years ago. A couple sought couples counseling. They were very embittered with each other but couldn't get a divorce because they had a dog that was the center of their lives, and neither of them was willing to give up even partial custody.

When we worked with them, we discovered that the wife resented her husband's habit of coming home from work, not even acknowledging her when he walked through the door, and directly heading upstairs to shower. By the time he arrived back downstairs, she would be so livid, they would get into a terrible argument.

We asked what the dog did that was different than what the wife did when the husband came home. It turned out the dog would run to the door, greet the husband, and get a nice rubbing in return. The wife would wait in the other room for the husband to seek her out, which he didn't do.

The husband complained that the wife was not physically affectionate. He longed for her to sit next to him on the couch while they were watching TV and cuddle up and kiss him. He would complain sarcastically that he must have body odor since she sat some distance from him.

We discovered that the dog was very assertive when he wanted affection. He would come over, sit next to the person from whom he wanted affection, push his front leg under their arm if they were distracted or unresponsive, and put his cold nose right on them until they petted him or snuggled with him.

It began to turn their relationship around to the point that they no longer wanted a divorce.

So we gave the couple this task: They were to study the dog and make him their teacher/guru. When they saw how he got what he wanted from their partner, they were to model that behavior and try it out with their partner. They had great fun with this, and it began to turn their relationship around to the point that they no longer wanted a divorce.

So this tip uses that idea. What animal could you model to help you shift your relationships in a positive or better direction? Be playful and creative with this one.

"Dog is your copilot," as the dyslexic's bumper sticker says.

The **Nicest** "No"

Learn to say "no." It will be
of more use to you
than to be able to read Latin.

—Charles H. Spurgeon

For years, I was too busy. I found myself saying yes to things I shouldn't have, partly to please people and partly to avoid missing an opportunity. I struggled for so many years to get people to say "yes" to me that saying "no" was difficult, even when I got too committed. I had to learn nice (and effective) ways of saying no.

> I struggled for so many years to get people to say "yes" to me that saying "no" was difficult.

The first "no" that began to work for me was not an absolute no, but a delay in my reflexive and automatic yes. I told people I would have to think about their request overnight and get back to them the next day. By then, I would usually be clear in my thinking and have a chance to work out what I would say if I was going to say no.

Next, I stumbled upon a "no" method that most people not only accepted but even seemed to encourage me to stick with, even when it disappointed or frustrated them:

I told them I was saying no because I was overly busy and

not spending enough time with my loved ones as I would like to and should. Most people responded with understanding and even admiration that I was so protective of my time with loved ones.

That leads to this change tip: Find the nicest and kindest ways to say no, and practice using at least one of them in the next week or so. If necessary, ask others you know who seem to be good at saying no in the kindest and most firm ways and model them or get them to tell you how they think about saying no and how they go about it.

Delibrate Mediocrity

Some men are born mediocre men,
some men achieve mediocrity,
and some men have mediocrity
thrust upon them.

—Joseph Heller

David Burns suggests that people who put pressure on themselves, who are perfectionistic, or who tend to be self-critical should give themselves a break by choosing to spend a "mediocre day." To do this, just operate at only 60 percent of your capacity all day, deliberately choosing to be mediocre.

People . . . should give themselves a break by choosing to spend a "mediocre day."

Try this one and find out what happens for you.

If You **Fall** on Your **Face**

People fail forward to success.

—Mary Kay Ash

My teacher, Milton Erickson, was fond of saying, "If you fall on your face, at least you are heading in the right direction." This saying has stuck with me all these years (since I first heard it in 1977), because I find it to be true in my life. I have gone a long way by allowing myself to make mistakes, be wrong, mess up, and generally keep moving forward. As the quote attributed to Winston Churchill says, "When you're going through hell, keep going."

R. H. Macy failed seven times before his store in New York caught on with the public.

English novelist John Creasey received 763 rejection slips before he published 564 books.

Babe Ruth struck out 1,330 times, but he also hit 714 home runs.

When I coach people on change, I notice a certain reluctance to step out, make mistakes, not know, be wrong, and fail. So this tip is to do something this week that you are not entirely sure you can do and commit yourself to being willing to fail, mess up, and not know. See if you can go beyond where you are or have been by stepping out of your comfort zone and into your area of incompetence.

The **Power** of **"and"**

The right word may be effective,
but no word was ever as
effective as a rightly timed pause.

—Mark Twain

Many years ago, I studied Gestalt therapy, which included a method that suggested to people that they substitute the word "and" for the word "but." For example, if you said something like, "I want to go to the beach, but I have to go to work," change it to, "I want to go to the beach *and* I have to go to work."

Pause and substitute the word "and" instead.

So this simple tip is: Change the doing by substituting "and" for "but." Whenever you notice yourself about to use the word "but," pause and substitute the word "and" instead.

Then notice how you experience changes (if any).

Here are some examples from therapist Brenda Dyer on how to use this tip in relationships. If you're having replays of power struggles in relational arguments or "discussions," try using the word "and" rather than "but." For example, "I really love you, *and* no." Or "I think that's a great point, *and* no." Or "Gee, that's an interesting way of looking at it, *and* I think I'll still do it my way."

From **Tense** to Getting the **Tenses Right**

The dogmas of the quiet past are
inadequate to the stormy present.
The occasion is piled high with difficulty, and we
must rise—with the occasion. As our case
is new, so we must think anew, and act anew.

—Abraham Lincoln

I once heard the founder of est (Erhard Seminars Training), Werner Erhard, speak about something he observed about people. He said it is like we have two filing cabinet drawers. One is labeled The Past. This is filled with everything that has happened to us, our history, genetic influences, traumas, joys, accomplishments, and so on. The other one is labeled The Future. This one, theoretically, should be empty, since the future has not happened yet.

Unfortunately, he noticed that many people's Future drawer is already filled with things from the past. This is when we project old ideas, fears, traumas, and so on into the future. People sometimes end up repeating patterns from the past.

This tip, suggested by counselor Paula Hanson, involves "getting the tenses right." She suggests that one should live a "grammatical" life: Get the tenses right. Let past events be in the past, leave the future till it comes, and acknowledge where you are: in the present.

If you find yourself speaking of something that occurred in the past in the present or future tense, or predicting the future, correct your verb tense, quietly bring yourself back to the present, and notice what is actually happening now.

Make a List and Check it Twice

I've been making a list of the things they don't teach you at school. They don't teach you how to love somebody. They don't teach you how to be famous. They don't teach you how to be rich or how to be poor. They don't teach you how to walk away from someone you don't love any longer. They don't teach you how to know what's going on in someone else's mind. They don't teach you what to say to someone who's dying. They don't teach you anything worth knowing.

—Neil Gaiman

Once, when I was unemployed, low on money, and starting to get depressed and discouraged, I sat down and made a list of everything I hadn't tried yet to get a job.

To my surprise, there were about twelve items on my list. I immediately felt more hope as I realized there were things I could do. I set about doing some of the things on my list, and before I got through three of them, I had landed a job.

I immediately felt more hope as I realized there were things I could do.

That leads to this change tip: When you are feeling frustrated or discouraged about something, sit down and make an honest list of things you could do to solve, resolve, or change the situation. If you get stuck and can't think of anything, ask a trusted friend or family member to help you come up with ideas.

Choose any item from the list and begin.

The
Opposite

When you discover you are
riding a dead horse, dismount.

—Dakota tribal wisdom

When I was a kid, I used to read *Superman* comics. There was a world featured in some of the comics called *Bizarro,* if memory serves me. In this world, everything was the opposite of what was true on Earth. To compliment someone, you insulted them. When you wanted to turn right, you turned left and ended up going right. There is a similar idea at play in an episode of the television series *Seinfeld*, when George decides that his instincts are always resulting in things he doesn't like, so he decides to do the opposite of whatever he feels is right—and he succeeds brilliantly.

She felt as if she were living the "Groundhog Day" of relationships, repeating the same thing over and over.

I heard a story from Susan Jeffers, the author of the bestseller *Feel the Fear and Do It Anyway* (Ballantine, 2006).She'd had a series of disastrous relationships. The men with whom she got involved seemed great at first, but later things went bad, and always in the same way. She felt as if she were living the *Groundhog Day* of relationships, repeating the same thing over and over. She was tired of it.

Around this time, a man to whom she wasn't attracted asked her out on a date. She initially refused but he persisted, and she finally agreed to go out on one date with him. During the date, she started to see some things about this man that initially weren't apparent to her and became interested enough to go out with him again. To make a long story short, she ended up marrying him. The moral of the story for her: Always date people who aren't your type. I wouldn't make the same conclusion in general, but in the situation she was in, there may be some wisdom in this notion.

This leads to this change tip: When you continue to be frustrated as you repeat personal or relationship patterns, do the opposite of what your instincts or feelings initially tell you to do.

Reclaiming Territory from Fear

I realize that if I wait until I am no longer
afraid to act, write, speak, be, I'll be sending
messages on an Ouija board, cryptic
complaints from the other side.

—Audre Lorde

This is a bit of a long one, but worth the few minutes it will take to read it, I think. When I was first in college, I developed a phobia of dogs, which led to a kind of agoraphobia. I rode my bicycle to the university from my house, and along the way, there were several mean dogs who would terrorize me by chasing me and trying to bite me while I was riding my bike. I only had a one-speed, and they would nip at me while I was peddling as fast as I could.

There were leash laws in the town, but the owners of these dogs ignored them, and I could never figure out which house to go to complain, since the dogs roamed in a pack in the neighborhood. I began to avoid going to classes unless I was able to leave at the same time as my older brother, who was attending law school. When I rode with him, the dogs would come nearby, but they would never attack us. He told me they never chased him when he rode alone. I began to believe that the dogs sensed my fear and that's why they targeted me. I would lie in bed at night fantasizing about killing one of these dogs, since they were making my life a misery and I was missing many classes.

One day, I decided to confront them. I jammed a big stick I found on the ground into my basket and, when the dogs came out to chase me, I jumped off the bike and swung the stick at them. They ran away—and off I rode to school. The same thing happened for the next week or so. I was terrified each time, but soon they just barked a little at me from a distance and never attacked. I was able to leave the stick at home and instead used my heavy bicycle chain and lock to swing at them when they came near on occasion. They never came close enough for me to hurt them (which was good for both of us; I didn't really want to hurt them). My fear subsided over time.

Some years later, a psychologist I knew brought one of his clients, a nineteen-year-old woman, to me for some help. They had worked together for a while, but with little success. She was desperately afraid of going too far from home because she feared if she were too far from a toilet, she would wet her pants. She had no medical condition that would make this likely, and it had never happened.

So the only places and ways she would leave home were typically to walk the two blocks to the community college she attended and when her mother would drive her. Because her mother would agree to stop immediately at any of the restrooms she had mapped out, she felt safe enough to go out occasionally with her mother.

I asked her about the best and worst moments in relationship to this problem and she told me two stories. One was when her father, who had divorced her mother and come out of the divorce negotiations financially much better, had offered to take her out for a birthday dinner on her nineteenth birthday. She told him she couldn't accept because her mother was working that evening and wouldn't be able to drive her.

He agreed to drive her and stop at any time, even though he thought this was contributing to her problem and he didn't approve of it. When she got into his car, dressed to the nines, she reminded him of his promise, but as soon as he could, he roared onto the freeway, which wasn't on her map. She became frightened and yelled at him to get off the freeway, but he only said, "I don't believe you will wet your pants. This is a ridiculous fear. I will give you five hundred dollars if you can pee on my new car seat right now."

She really wanted the money, was resentful that he could afford a new car when she and her mother were barely scraping by, and she also wanted to prove him wrong. But she discovered that not only could she not urinate, but the constant feeling of having to urinate disappeared for the entire evening. That was the best time.

The worst time, she told me, was when she had become frightened while watching a horror movie and demanded that her mother stay home from work because she was too frightened to be home alone. Her mother refused and drove off to work. The daughter became more and more panicked, until she was certain she would die from fright. She finally decided to end it all by running out the front door of the house, which she was certain would cause her heart to burst.

She ran out, still wearing her nightgown. But her heart didn't burst. She decided to run to the end of the front walk. Still, her heart, while beating wildly, didn't give out. She ran the entire two blocks to school, but still lived. She realized with embarrassment, finally, that she was standing in front of her school in her nightgown and quickly walked back home.

I told her she had stumbled on the solution to her problem but hadn't recognized it or taken it far enough. Fear, I told her, was like one of those electric fences they put around a yard to keep a dog in. The wire goes around the perimeter of the yard and shocks the dog through a collar if it approaches the edge of the yard. After several shocks, the dog learns to stay in the yard.

I explained to her that the fear was trying to keep her in a confined area, and that when she experienced freedom from her fear of urination that evening, she had, with the help of her father, jumped the invisible fence. She had jumped the fence again when she ran through her front door and to her college in her night-

Fear, I told her, was like one of those electric fences they put around a yard to keep a dog in.

gown. Now her task was to keep going and liberate more territory each day, each week, until she was free to move about the entire world.

And that leads to this change tip: freeing yourself from the restrictions of fear by reclaiming territory from fear. Where has fear stolen a little (or a lot) of your life, your free-dom, or your territory? What do you need to do to reclaim any (or all) of your territory or life from fear? What is the first step you can or will take to reclaim your territory? And when will you do this?

PART 2:

Change
the **Viewing**
Tips

Change Perspectives

If you want truly to understand
something, try to change it.

—Kurt Lewin

This tip involves getting a different perspective on a problem situation. Sometimes we get stuck with one view of the situation, which doesn't help us resolve it, get through it, or feel very good about it. Try one of the following tips to see if it makes a positive difference.

Think of the most optimistic person you know: How would he or she view this situation? Think of the most effective problem-solver you know: How would he or she view this situation? If it were five years from now, how do you think you'd be viewing this situation? Ten years? Twenty years? Fifty?

How could you turn this situation into some kind of artwork (such as the examples given in the following list) that would metaphorically express or illustrate the situation or your feelings about it or experience of it?

- A painting
- A memoir piece/autobiographical writing

- A poem
- A personal monologue given in front of an audience

- A sculpture
- A dance piece

- A song
- A photograph

- A short story

Notice or **Remember** Something **Different** or **Differently**

History does not repeat itself. But it rhymes.

—Mark Twain

Some years ago, while working with a man who had a fear of flying on airplanes, I observe that he kept going back to a scary moment on a flight several years prior to our work together. It was always the same moment: white knuckles clutching the seat in front of him, feeling the airplane bumping in the turbulent air, and feeling guilty for scaring the woman in the seat next to him with his talk about the plane going down.

When I asked him to broaden his memory and look around the plane to notice other things, he was surprised to notice that a woman a few rows up was calmly reading a book and that another man was sleeping like a baby. Noticing these other elements of the situation began to break the stranglehold this traumatic memory had on him, and his phobia began to ease a bit.

This tip involves noticing one thing about your situation you hadn't noticed before. There is a technique that has been used for years and made more formal within Neuro-linguistic Programming (NLP). It involves changing any of the sensory submodalities. Modalities are major modes of sensory processing (such as visual, auditory, tactile, olfactory, or gustatory) and submodalities are the different components within each modality (such as distance, color, sharp, dull, loud, soft, and so on) involved in your perception or memory of a problem situation. One of my favorite ones is imagining that a person who has said upsetting things to you has just inhaled helium and is speaking like Mickey Mouse. Or you might substitute Donald Duck, Howard Cosell, or James Cagney. Use your imagination. This is only one of the many modality shifts you can make in the auditory realm. You could speed up or slow down the sound or voice, imagine the sound running backward like a tape being rewound, and so on.

You could make changes in the visual submodalities as well. Again, you could speed up or slow down a movie of the scene. You could change the scene from color to black and white. You could put an overlay of purple on every scene. You could do the same thing using other modalities, but these are the most common.

So change any of the sensory aspects of your memory or perception to see whether or not this makes a positive difference for you.

Ask Different **Questions**

Judge a man by his questions
rather than by his answers.

—Voltaire

Sometimes when we experience trouble, we give ourselves more grief and trouble by asking the wrong questions. Some examples of questions that may lead to self-torture, or at least not help us resolve problems, could be:

- Why is this happening to me?

- Will this ever end?

- What did I do to deserve this?

- Why does this always happen to me?

- What is wrong with me?

Sometimes, instead of asking questions, we might frame our situation in the form of a statement, such as:

- I can't take it anymore.

- This is never going to end.

Here are a few suggestions for questions that might serve you better. If these don't fit or work, examine your current questions and discover or create better ones.

- Is this where I want to put my energy or attention? If not, where would I rather focus my energy or attention?

- Is there anything I can do about this right now? If so, what is the first step I will take? If not, how can I come to accept and make peace with what I can't change right now?

- What do I have to do to make it more the way I want it to be?

- What do I need to stop doing in order to have things be more the way I want them to be?

- If I'm going to have to go through this anyway, what can I get out of it?

- What are the facts and what are my stories/interpretations about the facts?

- What are the unhelpful stories and interpretations I have about the facts?

- Where are my moments or places of choice about this matter?

- What's the best way I've ever handled a situation like this?

Finding the Blessings in the Pain or the Problem

Man never made any material
as resilient as the human spirit.

—Bern Williams

This is a tip that you can only do for yourself (if you choose to). If you try to use it with someone else, it is likely to engender resentment. Ask yourself: *How could this situation, as hard and painful as it is, turn out to be a blessing in disguise?* Live in this question for a while. Your first answer may not be the best or final one.

Your first answer may not be the best or final one.

You Are the **Director**

You have to accept whatever comes,
and the only important thing is that
you meet it with the best you have to give.

—Eleanor Roosevelt

I had a client who would regularly get frustrated with the typical things her mother did and said. She would tensely anticipate a visit with her mother, and then after the visit, she would spend days seething over the things her mother had said or done. She practically had her mother's lines and actions memorized. I suggested she pretend that she was a movie producer trying to get her mother to act her part perfectly. When her mother delivered one of her classic lines with just the right tone, she should think to herself, *That was perfect. Cut!* She tried this and found herself laughing and enjoying the interaction rather than being upset by it. The bonus: her mother behaved a bit better (probably since my client wasn't reacting to her in the usual way).

Imagine that you have choreographed and arranged everything that happens.

As a thought experiment, imagine that you have choreographed and arranged everything that happens and everything that others do this week. Notice how that changes your sense of things.

Don't Expect; Be Happy

Life is a grindstone. Whether it grinds us down or polishes us up depends on us.

—L. Thomas Holdcroft

Ken Keyes developed a simple strategy to be happy. Expect everyone and everything to be exactly as it is. When you are upset, he suggests, it is only because your expectations haven't been fulfilled and you are demanding that reality be as you want it to be rather than how it is. So expect things to be as they are and you'll be happy.

For the next day or so, every time something happens within you or out in the world that could upset you, shift into expecting it to be exactly as it is. Tell yourself it is exactly as it is supposed to be.

Expect things to be as they are and you'll be happy.

Exhaust Your Inner Critic

To accuse others for one's own
misfortunes is a sign of want of education.
To accuse oneself shows that one's education
has begun. To accuse neither oneself nor others
shows that one's education is complete.

—Epictetus

Many years ago I read a book by Sondra Ray called *I Deserve Love* (Celestial Arts, 1995). It seemed a little hokey and New Age-y for my tastes, but it included a technique that I think can facilitate change, even if you don't buy the woo-woo philosophy upon which it is based.

Ray writes about a method of doing affirmations that goes beyond just repeating positive phrases to oneself (*Every day in every way, things are getting better and better.*). Here's her variation: Write out (or say out loud) a new belief or attitude you want to develop or incorporate, such as, *I now have a great and loving relationship,* or *I now have a career I love.* Insert your name into it to "reprogram" your unconscious mind. For example, *I, Bill, now have more than enough money, a flat stomach, and six-pack abs.* Do the affirmation using first person, second person, and third person pronouns: *I, Bill, now have more than enough money, a flat stomach, and six-pack abs. You, Bill, now have more than enough money, a flat stomach, and six-pack abs. He, Bill, now has more than enough money, a flat stomach, and six-pack abs.*

The idea behind using these three forms of address is that originally you "programmed" yourself by telling yourself (and believing) limiting or negative ideas, being told these beliefs by others, and/or by overhearing these beliefs discussed by others, so now you have to challenge these beliefs on these three levels.

But here's where we get beyond the woo-woo part if you don't buy the "reprogramming your unconscious" or "you create reality by your beliefs" bit. Every time you write or say the affirmation, dispute it. Let your mind come up with any objections: *No way. You've always handled money poorly, Bill, and will always be in debt, and you're in midlife, so you'll never be able to exercise enough to have a flat stomach or six-pack abs.* Or *I don't know. I like cheesecake and lying around reading a bit too much to be wealthy or svelte.* Or *This is just a bunch of New-Age tripe.* Or *This will never work.* Or *You're such a loser. This is a waste of time.* Keep going until your mind no longer has any new objections or until it falls silent. Once your inner critic is answered or exhausted, you can begin to make realistic affirming statements, such as, *I may not be as svelte as I was when I was younger, and I may not have as much money as I'd like, but I'm looking relatively good for my age, and I make a comfortable living that allows me to keep up with my bills.*

Where Do You Want to Put Your **Energy?**

It is the greatest of all mistakes
to do nothing because you can
only do a little. Do what you can.

—Sydney Smith

This is a simple tip. When you find yourself unhappy or dissatisfied, stop for a moment and ask yourself:

✓ Is this where I want to put my energy and attention right now?

✓ If it isn't, where or on what would I rather spend my time and attention?

Is this where I want to put my energy and attention right now?

✓ What do I need to do to shift in that preferred direction right now?

Use Others as Positive or Negative Models

Human beings, who are almost unique
in having the ability to learn from the
experience of others, are also remarkable
for their apparent disinclination to do so.

—Douglas Adams

The great thing about human beings is that we don't actually have to go through "learning experiences" personally. Recently scientists have identified "mirror neurons" that seem to fire off in our own brains when we observe others doing something.

Therefore, we can learn by observing and attending to others. This is why, despite our best efforts not to reproduce the worst of what we saw our parents do when we were children, we often end up acting exactly the way they did. But, of course, not everyone does this. Some people who had harsh and critical parents become loving and supportive parents. (Of course, it helps some if they were raised by two parents, and the other parent may have modeled different things.)

One of the implications of this is to be careful what you model and whom you observe carefully. There are two kinds of models: positive ones (those you want to emulate, who exhibit behaviors and beliefs that you would like to incorporate into your own life) and negative ones (those whose ways you want to avoid).

So this tip involves deliberately focusing on *both* kinds of mirrors. Spend some time doing the following while going about your everyday life: Find someone who does something well that you would like to be able to do. Observe them carefully and as often as you can. This person may only be on videotape or audiotape, or accessible through books or articles, and while that may work, it is best if you can get physical access to direct observation, since what people say isn't always the same as what they do. Observe where they put their attention. Observe their body movements. Observe the tone of voice they use. Observe how they interact with others, how they manage their time, how they deal with difficulties or set-backs, and anything else you notice.

Find someone who does something well that you would like to be able to do.

Then do the same with negative models. These are people who do not act the way you want to actor live the way you want to live. Observe them closely—their body movements, tone of voice, and so on—and determine from them what you don't want to do or be like.

Imagine You Have No Free Will

We are here and it is now.
Further than that, all human knowledge
is moonshine.

—H. L. Mencken

There is considerable experimental evidence that we are profoundly influenced by our environments and the language and metaphors that we and others use in a situation, and that we "decide" before we are conscious of having made a decision.

Sometimes it helps to imagine that you are not to blame.

If you are in a difficult situation, sometimes it helps to imagine that you are not to blame, because life just happens through you in the only way it could right now. This is not the old "you are doing the best you can with the resources and knowledge you have available right now" chestnut. This is actually more profound and radical. Life is "doing itself" through you, and you have the illusion of free will and control.

Now, I hasten to add that I am not claiming that this is true (although it may well be), only that it might be helpful. What if you weren't to blame, didn't decide, and this is just what's happening through you into life right now?

Reorient
to **Gratitude**

Instructions for having a life:

Pay attention.

Be astonished.

Tell about it.

—Mary Oliver, *Sometimes*

This is one I have found myself doing spontaneously lately, so I thought I would offer it in case you might want to try it out deliberately. I am writing this as the world is going through a challenging time economically. When I get dissatisfied or find myself complaining to myself or others, I reorient to the things for which I am grateful:

I live in a house.

I am not in foreclosure.

I have enough to eat.

I have friends and family who love me and whom I love.

I have hot and cold running water.

I have a car.

I have clean and nice clothes.

I have good health and the ability to move easily.

I am not in pain.

I find that washes of good feelings or at least contentment come to me as I reorient. Of course, your list might be different from mine. Give it a try and find out whether it makes a positive difference for you.

Be **Mindful** in Your **Relationships**

The best way to make your dreams
come true is to wake up.

—Paul Valéry

In *their study* "Mindfulness and Marital Satisfaction," Harvard professors of psychology Ellen Langer and Leslie Coates Burpee found that couples' relationships are more rewarding when partners use mindfulness to notice variations in their partners rather than generalizing by making comments such as, "You are always distracted" or "You are never spontaneous" (for the full article, see http://www.openground.com.au/articles/Mindf%20and%20Marital%20Satis.pdf).

So your assignment, should you accept it, is to note anything new about your partner, friend, family member, and/or coworker. It might be as simple as noting the color of their eyes. It might be noticing how they prepare their food. It might be noticing how they get dressed in detail. Anything you haven't really woken up to or noticed consciously might work. You might try to notice them doing something or being some way that is surprising to you or breaks your stereotyped or usual sense of them.

> Your assignment, should you accept it, is to note something new about your partner.

I Take
Exception

Nature provides exceptions to every rule.

—Margaret Fuller

We sometimes get trapped in certainty, in both our points of view and in our actions. One way to challenge this certainty, to ensure it is still up-to-date and helpful, is to search for and notice exceptions.

So, for the next week or so, I suggest that every time you have a particular thought, express a particular belief, or act in some typical way, think to yourself, *or not*; or *except when it's not that way*; or *except when I don't*; or *except when I am not that way*; or think of an exception to this rule or regularity. Or try doing something in your not-typical way, but rather in a way that is an exception to the rule.

Search for and notice exceptions.

You Are Not the Target

I can take any amount of criticism,
so long as it is unqualified praise.

—Noel Coward

Years ago I saw a Laura Huxley book with this title: *You Are Not the Target* (Perseus Books, 1998). I never actually read it, but it stuck in my mind and leads to this week's tip. Sometimes in life, people get upset with us, blame us, shame us, get angry with us, and so on. This may be hard to handle. You may feel bad, anxious, and upset, and respond in a similar manner to this kind of thing.

Imagine you are not the target.

So, the tip is: Imagine you are not the target. The person is experiencing something difficult within him- or herself and is attributing that difficult thing to you. Have compassion for their struggle rather than being defensive or hurt by their critique or attack.

How would you respond to someone who is hurt, frightened, struggling, or upset? Do the best you can to respond while keeping this in mind, without being patronizing or condescending. Now, I'm not saying if they get physically violent, just shift your point of view. I am talking about shifting your response to things they do or say that are not physically threatening.

What if you aren't the target?

Dissolving Upsets

My young son asked me what happens
after we die. I told him we get buried
under a bunch of dirt and worms eat our bodies.
I guess I should have told him the truth—that
most of us go to Hell and burn eternally—
but I didn't want to upset him.

—Jack Handy

I went through est training in the 1970s. They didn't allow note taking, but at one point they said something that I found so helpful, I memorized it. There are three elements to upsets (est practitioners and seminar leaders often turned emotions and states of mind from verbs into nouns):

1. Unfulfilled expectations
2. Thwarted intentions
3. Undelivered communications

That leaves us with four areas to examine whenever we get upset.

I thought this covered the waterfront, but in recent years, I have added one more of my own:

4. Unrealized truths about oneself, others, the world, or life.

So that leaves us with four areas to examine whenever we get upset about something or at someone. When you find yourself upset, you could ask:

- What did I expect that didn't happen?

- Can I let go of that expectation and get with the way things are instead?

- Where did any of my intentions get thwarted?

- Is there another way to realize that intention?

- Could or should I give up that intention?

- What haven't I said or communicated to someone in this situation?

- What am I afraid to say?

- How could I get myself to communicate or say what needs to be communicated in the most truthful and most compassionate way?

- What truth haven't I acknowledged in this situation?

- What is standing in the way of that acknowledgment?

- How can I get myself to acknowledge that truth?

Remember to **Forget**

The true art of memory is the art of attention.

—Samuel Johnson

Forget bad and intrusive memories by shifting focus from traumatic and bad memories to other thoughts. Once you have told your story, either out loud or on paper, each time the unpleasant thought intrudes upon you, shift your thoughts to any other subject that is not unpleasant. Do this until the unpleasant memories or thoughts become less frequent or intrusive.

Shift your thoughts to any other subject that is not unpleasant.

Take Your Own Best Advice

We should be careful and discriminating
in all the advice we give. We should be especially
careful in giving advice that we would not think
of following ourselves. Most of all, we ought to
avoid giving counsel which we don't follow when
it damages those who take us at our word.

—Adlai Stevenson

I was once doing therapy with a teenager who kept getting into fights and getting kicked out of high school. He really didn't want to see a therapist (his parents and the school insisted). He told me that when someone "dissed" him, he had to react and fight or no one would respect him.

He should take a breath, count to ten, and think about the consequences before he acts.

After I had been seeing him in therapy for some time (and getting nowhere), I had another teen referred to me from a different high school who was also getting into fights regularly and getting suspended from school. I told my current client about getting this new referral and asked him to give me some hints about what to tell the other teen, since my client was an expert in this issue. He suggested I tell the other boy that he should think before he reacted. I asked how to respond if the other boy said he just reacted and couldn't think. He said, "Then he should take a breath, count to ten, and think about

114 | The Change Your Life Book

the consequences before he acts. He should think about how mad his parents and the school were going to be and that he would have to see a shrink like you."

I discussed this advice with the new client when he arrived in therapy and he was unmoved by it, but the first boy came back and reported that he hadn't gotten into one fight that week. When I asked him how he managed that, he said, "It was easy. I took a breath and counted to ten."

This leads to this change tip: What would you say to someone facing the same issue or problem you are facing? What advice would you give them? And can you implement any of that advice in your own life?

Becoming a
Not-Know-It-All

Before I got married I had six theories
about bringing up children;
now I have six children and no theories.

—John Wilmot, 2nd Earl of Rochester

The other day I heard a speaker say that she was a Not-Know-It-All. That tickled me and seemed like a great place to end these change tips. One of my favorite stories is about the parenting expert who created ten useful principles that he taught to parents on how to do better in their roles of raising their children. He gave classes that were well attended and popular. He called these classes "Ten Commandments for Parents."

He didn't have any children himself, but after teaching the class for a few years, he met the woman of his dreams and they had a child together. After being a parent for one year, he decided to rename the class "Five Suggestions for Parents." After another child and another year, he retitled the class "Three Tentative Hints for Parents." After he and his wife were blessed with twins, he stopped teaching all together.

So, I'll leave you with this last "Change the Viewing" tip: Whenever you are certain of something, but things aren't going well, embrace not knowing and instead become uncertain. Especially challenge those long-held immutable truths and beliefs.

The story is told of the farmer in China whose luck

seemed to be taking a turn for the better when a wild horse ran into his yard and stayed for a bite to eat, then became an extra horse when the man's son tamed him. In this very poor region of China, this was a blessing. When the neighbors told the man he was blessed, he said, "Maybe so, maybe not." The neighbors could not understand how he could say such a thing. Surely this was a good thing.

Sometime later, his son was riding the horse and fell off and broke his leg. The neighbor's came by to express their sympathy. "What a terrible thing has happened. Your son will not be able to help you with the harvest and some of your crops will spoil." He only replied calmly, "Perhaps it was a tragedy, perhaps not." Again, they found this response strange and nonsensical. Of course it was a tragedy.

A short while later, the emperor's army came riding through the village and conscripted every able-bodied young man for a battle in which they were sure to die. The neighbor's, now seeing the man's wisdom, said, "You were right. Your son's broken leg has saved his life. It was not a tragedy at all. It was really a blessing in disguise." The man again replied, "Maybe so; perhaps not."

PART 3:

Change the Setting Tips

Change Locations

Man's heart away from nature becomes hard.

—Standing Bear

A colleague in Australia suggests that couples who are having the same old conflicts go for a walk in the woods and have the discussion or disagreement there. They often report a significant change in the conversation due to the different setting.

This leads to this suggestion: Try changing the physical location or setting for recurring problems.

> They often report a significant change in the conversation due to the different setting.

Change the Timing

In order to be successful, all you've
got to do is to show up 80 percent of the time.

—Woody Allen

Try this: Schedule your problem for a certain time of day or evening. Limit the time of the problem (e.g, set a timer and argue for five minutes only, followed by five minutes of silence; worry for ten minutes every night; and so on).

Schedule your problem.

The **Tape Recorder** Cure

I was going to buy a copy of
The Power of Positive Thinking,
and then I thought:
What the hell good would that do?

—Ronnie Shakes

One time a woman came to me and told me that she thought her daughter was mean and out of control. The daughter would misbehave and defy her mother every chance she got unless her father was around—then she acted just fine. So the father was against bringing the girl in for counseling, but her mother was at her wit's end. I suggested that the mother audiotape interactions between her and her daughter and then bring me the tape.

Long story short: The mother discovered that as soon as she turned the tape recorder on, the daughter would either clam up or behave better, so she began to use the tape to interrupt their conflicts. The mother also noticed that she herself also acted and spoke more calmly when the tape recorder was running.

This leads to this suggestion: Try audiotaping or video-taping some problematic situation. If there are others involved, inform them that the taping is happening. Listen to or watch the tape afterward.

Subsize **Me**

The most remarkable thing
about my mother is that for thirty years
she served the family nothing but leftovers.
The original meal has never been found.

—Calvin Trillin

I read a piece of research recently about the effects of smaller and bigger dinner plates on people's eating habits. Researchers Brian Wansink and Koert van Ittersum discovered that switching from a twelve-inch to a ten-inch dinner plate led people to serve and eat 22 percent less food ("The Perils of Plate Size: Waist, Waste, and Wallet," *Journal of Marketing* [2008]; available at www.small-platemovement.org/doc/big_bowls.doc).

This leads to this tip: Try eating from smaller containers for a week or so. If you are at a restaurant for a meal, take part of the main dish or the side dishes off the main plate and put them on a side plate (ask for one if there isn't one on the table).

Switching from a twelve-inch to a ten-inch dinner plate led people to serve and eat 22 percent less food.

Allies for **Change**

May we be fearless . . . from friends
and enemies . . . from known
and unknown . . . from night and day . . .
May all the directions be our allies.

—Atharva Veda

This tip comes from a suggestion by Marcia Rutland, from British Columbia (thanks, Marcia!). Ask a friend, relative, or colleague to be your "change ally" for the week. Choose a reasonable but procrastinated or challenging goal to accomplish for the week, and have your ally do the same.

Every day/evening, e-mail or phone each other to let your ally know what you have accomplished that day toward your goal. Or, if daily is too much, e-mail, call, or visit each other at the end of the week to check in about what you have accomplished.

Marcia gives a couple of nice examples of how this worked for her: "A friend and I agreed to our own daily goals. He would put five things on eBay per night to clear out his stuff and make some money. I agreed to close two EAP [Employee Assistance Program] client files per night. We e-mailed nightly. It was actually fun and was competition to see who would e-mail first! Another ally spent one hour per week helping me declutter my spare room, and I helped her make decisions regarding her clothing, which she tried on for me, and decluttered her closet. We set the dates and times each week, finished in no time, and had fun too."

Rearrange
the Furniture

Shin: Device for finding furniture in the dark.

—Brenda Dyer

This change tip was suggested by therapist Brenda Dyer. It's a simple tip, but try it and you may be surprised to discover how powerful it can be. When you're feeling bogged down or indecisive, go home and rearrange the furniture in one of your rooms. Literally resituate the chairs, desks, lamps, and so on. You'll be surprised at how this gives you a different perspective.

So, there **you** have it. A **changed life** in one year. And **all** by making **small changes** weekly.

I suspect by now you have gotten the spirit of these tips and might even come up with your own in the future.

Another tip, one that I discovered as I was reading the final version of this book: I discovered that I had forgotten some of the tips, even though I came up with them and wrote them myself. So that leads to my final hint: Every once in a while, read this book (or just dip into a tip or two) again. You may be surprised to rediscover some idea or change that may be just the one you need in your life at that moment.

Thank you for coming along on this "Change Your Life" ride.

Acknowledgments

These tips first appeared in a series of e-mail tips I shared via my website. I could only think of forty and I wanted fifty-two, one for each week in a year. I put out the call and was overwhelmed with the response. I couldn't and didn't use all the ideas that were sent, but it got me going and I wrote the last twelve.

I specifically used some terrific ideas that I got from these generous people. Thank you, all. I couldn't have done it without you: Marcia Rutland, Barbara Hunt, Paula Hanson, Diane Boisjoli, and Brenda Dyer.

Another person I couldn't have done it without was Harold Dumanig, my extraordinary assistant, who made the

initial version of this book all come together and look good.
Thank you, Harold.

And to Sandy Beadle, friend, coauthor of a previous book,
and e-book maven: the previous edition wouldn't have happened without you and your patient persistence and willing-
ness to be a lifelong learner.

And finally to all the folks at HCI who shepherded the
version you are holding in your hands into the world with
kindness and professionalism.

About the Author

Bill O'Hanlon, M.S., LMFT, has authored or coauthored over thirty books, including *The Therapist's Notebook on Positive Psychology, Quick Steps to Resolving Trauma, A Guide to Trance Land, Pathways to Spirituality, Change 101*, and *Thriving Through Crisis*, which won a Books for a Better Life Award. His books have been translated into fifteen languages. He has appeared on a variety of radio and television programs, including *Oprah* and *Today*. A top-rated presenter at many national conferences since 1977, Bill has given more than 3,000 talks around the world and was selected as the Outstanding Mental Health Educator of the Year in 2001 by the New England Educational Institute. Bill is a licensed mental health professional, certified professional counselor, and a licensed marriage and family therapist. He is a clinical member of the American Association for Marriage and Family Therapy (AAMFT) and winner of the 2003 New Mexico AAMFT Distinguished Service Award, certified by the National Board of Certified Clinical Hypnotherapists, and a Fellow and a board member of the American Psychotherapy Association, by whom he was recognized in 2008 for outstanding dedication and commitment to the mental health field. He is known for his storytelling, irreverent humor, clear and accessible style, and his boundless enthusiasm for whatever he is doing. Learn more at www.ChangeYourLifeBook.com.